FINAL
VICTORY

FINAL VICTORY

Contemplating the Death and Funeral of a Christian

BRYAN WOLFMUELLER

CONCORDIA PUBLISHING HOUSE • SAINT LOUIS

CONTENTS

TALKING ABOUT DEATH AND DYING

Precious in the sight of the LORD is the death of His saints.
Psalm 116:15

"Two things are certain," as the saying goes, "death and taxes." This is true, at least of death. The mortality rate is 100 percent. Unless we are alive on Judgment Day, we will all experience death.

For an event so common, death remains a difficult subject to discuss. When a loved one dies, it is often accompanied by pain, sickness, or even tragedy. Sadness, grief, and sorrow then follow. Death hurts. Compound this with our society's tendency to hide death and mask sickness, and you have a recipe for avoidance.

Many families, when they see that death is drawing near for a loved one, refuse to acknowledge it. Even some people on their own deathbeds pretend that everything is okay and that they will soon be healthy again. Now, it is true that there is health and new life on the other side of death, but the jarring reality has to be faced: "You are dying." Even if you are young and healthy as you read this book, the same thing is true. You are dying. All of us are.

As Christians, we do not avoid the difficulties of this life but face them head-on with the truth of Scripture. When we speak of death and dying, we acknowledge that there is something wrong in the world, even something wrong with us. But Jesus has provided the solution for these problems, for death and the sin that causes it. He knows what it is like to die, to be laid in a tomb, and to be alive again. Although we are marching toward the grave, Jesus has given us the promise that death has lost its sting and that there is life on the other side of the grave.

What follows in this book is offered with the prayer that in hearing what the Scriptures have to say about death, we would approach our own graves with a confident faith in our Lord Jesus, saying with St. Paul, "For me to live is Christ, and to die is gain" (Philippians 1:21).

INTRODUCTION

Some say that talking about death is the hardest discussion to have. Why is this? Are we afraid that acknowledging death will make it arrive sooner? Are we avoiding the painful emotions that often accompany this discussion? Has the death of a loved one left unresolved questions and emotions? The answer is most likely yes to all these questions.

Few reach adulthood without having experienced a loss of some kind. Certainly few emerge from their thirties without experiencing the death of a family member, friend, co-worker, close acquaintance, or pet. No one is immune to loss and the resulting grief. While there are differences in the ways individuals experience and cope with loss, there are many similarities that can help those who survive learn to process their loss.

Whether you are a lifelong Lutheran or a new Christian, you will find in these brief pages tools that provide a Christian understanding of death. An important element of this understanding is the Christian funeral service, a rite often called the Burial of the Dead. The funeral service becomes for the Christian a witness of one's faith. As such, it is desirable to have the funeral reflect what Scripture believes, teaches, and confesses about the death of a believer.

This book can also serve as a resource to help an individual or family plan for a Christian funeral. The days that follow a death are tumultuous and emotional. Preplanning removes some of the necessary decisions to a time that is less hurried and less emotional. While preplanning a funeral seems morbid to some, it is actually a loving and caring act for those who will survive.

PRAYER TO ACCEPT GOD'S WILL

O God of grace and mercy, I thank You for Your loving-kindness shown to all Your servants, who having finished their course in faith, now rest from their labors. Grant me grace to say with a believing heart, "Thy will be done," and know that Your will, though often hidden, is good and gracious. Strengthen me through Your Word and Sacraments for that day when You will call me to Yourself, that I may also be faithful unto death, joyfully receive the crown of eternal life, and join the whole company of heaven to live with You forever. *Amen.*

LIFE, DEATH, AND THE RESURRECTION

For the wages of sin is death, but the free gift of God is eternal life in Christ Jesus our Lord. *Romans 6:23*

THE CAUSE OF DEATH

Death was not part of God's original creation. In the first chapter of Genesis, we hear the wonderful refrains "It was good" and "It was very good." Life was flourishing! Death was not part of God's good creation.

How, then, did death begin? After God created Adam and Eve, He placed them in the Garden of Eden and gave them "dominion over the fish of the sea and over the birds of the heavens and over every living thing that moves on the earth" (Genesis 1:28). In the midst of the garden, God planted the tree of life and the tree of the knowledge of good and evil. God commanded Adam and Eve: "You may surely eat of every tree of the garden but of the tree of the knowledge of good and evil you shall not eat, for in the day that you eat of it you shall surely die" (Genesis 2:16–17). Tempted by Satan to doubt God's Word and to desire what was forbidden them, Adam and Eve sinned by eating from the forbidden tree. Because Adam listened to Eve and ate of the tree that God had commanded him not to eat, Adam, and all humankind after him, is cursed to labor for the bread he eats "till you return to the ground, for out of it you were taken; for you are dust, and to dust you shall return" (Genesis 3:19). The Scriptures go on to record,

Then the LORD God said, "Behold, the man has become like one of Us in knowing good and evil. Now, lest he reach out his hand and take also of the tree of life and eat, and live forever—" therefore the LORD God sent him out from the garden of Eden to work the ground from which he was taken. He drove out the man, and at the east of the garden of Eden He placed the cherubim and a flaming sword that turned every way to guard the way to the tree of life. (Genesis 3:22–28)

Every human being born since, every one a descendant of Adam, has an inheritance of sin and death. Each of us is a sinner. Each of us, then, will die. Death is the judgment for our sin, as Scripture tells us: "The wages of sin is death" (Romans 6:23; see also James 1:15). This is why death is such a fearful thing. It is the punishment for our sin, and on the other side of death, we face condemnation and judgment for our sin.

Sin came into the world through one man, and death through sin, and so death spread to all men because all sinned. (Romans 5:12)

There is nothing that we can do to eliminate death. There is no human accomplishment, effort, or ingenuity that can beat back death and give man immortality. Until the Lord returns, every single person will die. We all need a Savior to rescue us from death.

"O death, where is your victory? O death, where is your sting?"

The sting of death is sin, and the power of sin is the law. But thanks be to God, who gives us the victory through our Lord Jesus Christ. (1 Corinthians 15:55–57)

THE DEATH OF JESUS

Death has a claim on all of us because of our sin. But Jesus had no sin, and so the grave had no claim on Him. Death went too far when it took hold of Jesus, and death lost its claim on all humanity. Death is destroyed. Jesus takes upon Himself our death, the punishment for our sins, the condemnation that we deserve, and the wrath of God that our sin had kindled. He took it on Himself so that our death no longer forever separates us from God. The Lord gives us salvation in the place of condemnation and forgiveness in the place of judgment—life in the place of death.

We still experience death, but we now have new life in Christ. And the life we now live is freed from the fear of our own death, because in Jesus we know that death is not the last word. We have this explained beautifully in Hebrews:

Since therefore the children share in flesh and blood [we have mortal bodies], [Jesus] Himself likewise partook of the same things [in His incarnation, taking on our humanity], that through death He might destroy the one who has the power of death, that is, the devil, and deliver all those who through fear of death were subject to lifelong slavery. (Hebrews 2:14–15)

All of this is manifest before the world in the Lord's resurrection. When He came out of the grave on the third day, the reign of death ended. Before the resurrection, the grave could have been marked with a sign: "One Way—No Way Out." But Jesus turns and walks out of the grave. He makes a way through death. Jesus' resurrection proves that death's grip is broken, that the grave is not the end, and that all flesh will rise on the Last Day.

In the death and resurrection of our Lord Jesus, we have the fulfillment of this great promise:

And He will swallow up on this mountain the covering that is cast over all peoples, the veil that is spread over all nations. He will swallow up death forever; and the Lord GOD will wipe away tears from all faces, and the reproach of His people He will take away from all the earth, for the LORD has spoken. It will be said on that day, "Behold, this is our God; we have waited for Him, that He might save us. This is the LORD; we have waited for Him; let us be glad and rejoice in His salvation." (Isaiah 25:7–9)

THE CHRISTIAN'S DEATH

Death is our enemy, but it is our destroyed enemy. This understanding, this paradox, determines our attitude, as Christians, toward dying. Like Jesus, we do not simply accept death as something good or natural or inevitable. We do not need to "come to grips" with dying, with being sick, or with getting old. Death is and will remain our enemy. But because of Jesus' death, we realize that death has no power over us, that the grave is nothing to fear, that all the darkness of the tomb has been replaced by the radiance of Jesus' resurrection. We face our own death in the confidence of our faith, knowing that death is defeated. On the other side of death, our Lord Jesus has for us eternal life and salvation.

On His way to raise Lazarus, who had been dead for four days, Jesus is met by Martha. In the midst of her tears, Jesus teaches her about life, death, and the resurrection. The words of comfort that Jesus spoke to Martha are also for us and our comfort: "Jesus said to her, 'I am the resurrection and the life. Whoever believes in Me, though he die, yet shall he live, and everyone who lives and believes in Me shall never die' " (John 11:25–26).

Because of Jesus and His death, because He took all the punishment for our sin, because all of our sins are forgiven, and because we are His people, marked with His name in our Baptism, we have nothing to fear in death. Faith knows that Jesus brings us death as a gift. This is a mystery: just as Jesus destroyed death by dying, so He gives His Christians life through their death. Though we die, yet we shall live. For the Christian, death is the final answer to our daily petition in the Lord's Prayer, "Deliver us from evil." When we die, we will pray that prayer no more; it will be answered. Our death is a gift from Jesus to bring us from death to life.

This is why the Scriptures give such soft and kind names to the death of a Christian. The Church Fathers called these the "sweet names of death."

THE SWEET NAMES OF DEATH

1. "Gathered to his people" (Genesis 25:8, 17)

In the Old Testament especially, we see the hope of being gathered to one's people. Such is our hope today. Death tears people apart—husbands from wives, parents from children, friends from one another. So we cling to the sure promise that we will be reunited with all our dearly departed in the life to come.

2. "Depart and be with Christ" (Philippians 1:23)

This is the Christian's great desire: to be with the Lord. We have the Lord's promise that He has gone to prepare a place for us, that where He is, we will be also (John 14:1–4). One of the most beautiful pictures of eternal life is in the last chapter of the Bible: "They will see His face" (Revelation 22:4a). When we close our eyes in death, we will open them to see the beautiful face of our Savior and our friend Jesus Christ.

3. "Depart in peace" (Luke 2:29)

Simeon held Jesus in his hands, saw with his own eyes the salvation of the world, and then was ready to die in peace. This peace is the peace that we have with God because of the forgiveness of all our sins (Romans 5:1). There is no fear of judgment or condemnation in death, because we have the Lord's gift of eternal peace.

4. "Taken away from calamity" (Isaiah 57:1)

There is sin, death, temptation, and sadness around every turn in this world, even inside of us. When we die, our soul will be finally free from sin. The stain of original sin, which is forgiven in Baptism, will also be removed in death. When the Lord gives us death, He takes us out of this veil of tears and brings us into His glory and perfection. Because of Jesus and His cross, our death is a blessed event. We permanently leave behind death and every evil and know nothing but the Lord's goodness.

5. **"Sleep"** (Matthew 9:24; John 11:11; 1 Thessalonians 4:13;
   1 Corinthians 15:18)

Jesus first calls death "sleep," and this is certainly one of the sweetest names of death. Sleep implies waking up! This is what Jesus meant when He said to the mourners, "Go away, for the girl is not dead but sleeping" (Matthew 9:24). In this we see what Jesus plans to do. He "went in and took her by the hand, and the girl arose" (Matthew 9:25). The same is true of Lazarus. Jesus explains this in a conversation with His disciples:

He said to them, "Our friend Lazarus has fallen asleep, but I go to awaken him."

The disciples said to Him, "Lord, if he has fallen asleep, he will recover."

Now Jesus had spoken of His death, but they thought that He meant taking rest in sleep. Then Jesus told them plainly, "Lazarus has died, and for your sake I am glad that I was not there, so that you may believe. But let us go to him." (John 11:11–15)

Just like waking follows sleep, so the resurrection follows death. When the Scriptures call our death "sleep," they are putting before us the great hope of the resurrection of the body and life everlasting. By faith in the Lord's forgiveness, we fear the grave as little as our bed (*LSB* 883:3).

6. **"Passed from death to life"** (John 5:24; see also 2 Timothy 1:10;
   Revelation 2:10)

This is backward, at least to our own experience. To us it looks like death comes after life, but not in the kingdom of God! Life comes after death. In a wonderful way, this already applies to the baptized. We have already died with Jesus (Romans 6:1–4), and the life we now live is one we live by faith in Him (Galatians 2:20). All who trust in Jesus have eternal life right now (John 3:16) and have already passed from death to life. When we die, then, we finally leave death behind and enter into life eternal.

7. "Deliverance from evil" (see Matthew 6:13)

Every time we pray the Lord's Prayer, we ask the Lord for a blessed death and the life eternal that comes after death. Martin Luther explains: "We pray in this petition, in summary, that our Father in heaven would rescue us from every evil of body and soul, possessions and reputation, and finally, when our last hour comes, give us a blessed end, and graciously take us from this valley of sorrow to Himself in heaven" (Small Catechism, Seventh Petition).

8. "Gain" (Philippians 1:21)

Much of the literature about death is focused on loss—"Losing Someone You Love," "Handling the Loss of a Child," and so on. But here St. Paul gives us the blessed opposite. He calls death "gain." The blessedness of the saints in heaven confirms this wonderful understanding. The treasures of the kingdom of God and His righteousness and blessedness and holiness, which we hold now by faith, we will hold then with our eyes and hands. We will have the fullness of the gracious inheritance left for us by Jesus: life, salvation, and the forgiveness of all sin.

There is a faithful longing for death in the hearts of the Lord's people. We know that we are pilgrims and strangers in this world and that our true home is in the presence of our beloved brother, Jesus. We know that He is with us now in our trouble, but we long, with St. Paul, to depart for that better place.

The Holy Spirit has given us a catalog of comfort here. When we think and speak of death in these ways, our faith is strengthened to face death, both our own and our neighbor's. When we think of death in this way, we learn how to mourn with hope and joy.

MOURNING WITH HOPE

If, because of Christ, death is such a blessed event, should Christians mourn?

Dying people instruct their families: "Do not cry for me. Do not be sad." The sentiment is understandable—the dying do not want to hurt their family or make them sad, and they want to give their family confidence that they will be in a better place. But death is sad. It hurts. The trouble with the injunction on crying is that it can make things worse. You feel sad because your friend died, and then you feel sad because you were told not to be.

Death is still our enemy. Even Jesus wept when He heard that His friend Lazarus was dead, and Jesus knew that He would raise Lazarus from the dead. The shortest verse in the Bible tells us about Jesus' tears over death: "Jesus wept" (John 11:35). So should we. We mourn death; we are sad when our loved ones die. There is no shame in our suffering.

But we must remember that death is still defeated. We are not given over to despair. We mourn with joy. We cry with laughter. Our tears are mixed with hope. In the shadow of the grave, we sing of life eternal. In the midst of death, we confess the resurrection. We mourn with hope.

We do not want you to be uninformed, brothers, about those who are asleep, that you may not grieve as others do who have no hope. For since we believe that Jesus died and rose again, even so, through Jesus, God will bring with Him those who have fallen asleep. (1 Thessalonians 4:13–14)

THE GREAT HOPE OF THE RESURRECTION

On the Day of Judgment, the Lord Jesus will return to the earth and call all people out of their graves and give the resurrection to all flesh (believer and unbeliever alike). For the unbeliever, this is a resurrection unto death (in the worst paradox imaginable). For believers in Christ, this is the resurrection unto life (see John 5:25–29). Just as the soul is set free from the corruption of sin when we die, our bodies are set free from the corruption and bondage of sin in the resurrection. "Our citizenship is in heaven, and from it we await a Savior, the Lord Jesus Christ, *who will transform our lowly body to be like His glorious body*, by the power that enables Him even to subject all things to Himself" (Philippians 3:20–21, emphasis added).

St. Paul shows us the importance and the great benefits of the resurrection in 1 Corinthians 15 (often referred to as "The Resurrection Chapter"). This chapter gives us comfort in the face of death, the joyous expectation of this corruption putting on incorruption and our mortality putting on immortality.

So is it with the resurrection of the dead. What is sown is perishable; what is raised is imperishable. It is sown in dishonor; it is raised in glory. It is sown in weakness; it is raised in power. It is sown a natural body; it is raised a spiritual body. If there is a natural body, there is also a spiritual body. Thus it is written, "The first man Adam became a living being"; the last Adam became a life-giving spirit. But it is not the spiritual that is first but the natural, and then the spiritual. The first man was from the earth, a man of dust; the second man is from heaven. As was the man of dust, so also are those who are of the dust, and as is the man of heaven, so also are those who are of heaven. Just as we have borne the image of the man of dust, we shall also bear the image of the man of heaven. (1 Corinthians 15:42–49)

After the resurrection, the Scriptures tell us about the "new heavens and a new earth." "But according to His promise we are waiting for new heavens and a new earth in which righteousness dwells" (2 Peter 3:13; see also 1 John 3:2–3; Revelation 21:1–8). This promise is the solid foundation of our faith and hope. We will dwell there eternally in the face of our Savior Jesus (Revelation 22:4) because He, in His mercy and love and in His suffering and blood, has declared us to be righteous and holy.

If it were left to us to fight against death, we would have no hope, no chance. By our own efforts we cannot dispel the gloom of the grave. Through our own works we cannot escape the sting of death, sin, or the judgment that is to follow.

But praise be to our Lord Jesus Christ who has done the work for us, died in our place, carried our condemnation, and forgiven our sins. Because our Jesus has taken up the fight against death and won, we live and die with a full confidence that we are the Lord's. He has for us the gift of the resurrection of the body and life everlasting.

CONSIDER

How do the "sweet names of death" listed earlier comfort you? How might you use these passages to comfort others?

How does Jesus' death give us hope?

CHRISTIAN BURIAL: THROUGH DEATH TO LIFE

Do you not know that all of us who have been baptized into Christ Jesus were baptized into His death? We were buried therefore with Him by baptism into death, in order that, just as Christ was raised from the dead by the glory of the Father, we too might walk in newness of life. *1 Thessalonians 4:13b*

As discussed in the previous section, death is a consequence of the fall into sin (Genesis 3:19; Romans 5:12). The coming of life incarnate into our world signals the death of death and the ultimate victory of life. Jesus meets death and grief head-on (Luke 7:1–17; Mark 5:35–43; John 11:1–44) and transforms them by His own death, burial, and resurrection, thus giving way to life.

In Holy Baptism, we are immersed in Christ's death, burial, and resurrection (Romans 6:3–11). Luther says that one's burial and resurrection from the dead are the fulfillment of one's Baptism: "This journey (from this life to the life beyond) begins in Baptism. And as long as there is faith, man continues on this course until he completes it through death." The burial rites themselves are a kind of journey that begins at the deathbed, leads to the funeral home and the church, and finally to the cemetery. They follow the believer as he or she departs this world with Christ through death to life.

CHRISTIAN BURIAL: THROUGH DEATH TO LIFE

BURIAL RITES

In the burial rites, two emphases are held in tension: penitence and the resurrection (2 Samuel 12:15–23). The Kyrie, Litany, penitential psalms, and the ancient Christian hymn "In the Very Midst of Life" (*LSB* 755) are examples of how the rites take seriously both death and the deep effect death has on us. In Christ, the sting of death is conquered so that the Christian sees, in the midst of death, the hope of the resurrection of the body and life everlasting. The various Scripture readings, hymnody, and the prayers in the rites testify to the glorious victory over death that is ours in Christ Jesus our Lord.

Deathbeds have been the time of confession both of the faith and of the resurrection of the body. Christ calls death a sleep (Mark 5:39) and so, for Christians, the hour of death can be approached with the confidence of falling asleep. The **Commendation of the Dying** offers comfort to Christians as they see their dying in the light of their Savior's death. The rite offers the opportunity for confession of the faith as well as the confession of sins before death. For the family, the rite assists them in making the transition from having their loved one with them to seeing him or her in the arms of their gracious Savior.

Upon hearing the news of a death, many people come to extend their consolation to the family and share in their grief. The rite of **Comforting of the Bereaved** gives a structure for the pastor to comfort "those who are in any affliction" (2 Corinthians 1:4) with the Word of God. Most often, this rite occurs at the funeral home.

The **Funeral Service** is a public service of the Church. It is a public confession of the faith concerning death, burial, resurrection, and the life hereafter. The baptismal theme of death and resurrection with Christ is most prominent (Romans 6:1–11). The funeral service, then, is the public proclamation of the marvelous and gracious works of our great God and Savior, Jesus, applied to this specific situation. In the service, we join the saints and angels, the Church in heaven and on earth, in giving thanks to the Lord Jesus for the gifts He has won and delivered to us in His death and for the comfort Christians find in the resurrection.

The body is God's creation. God Himself took on flesh and bone in Jesus to redeem the world. The Holy Spirit sanctifies the Christian, body and soul, in Baptism, in the hearing of God's Word, and in the communion of Christ's life-giving body and blood in the Sacrament. For this reason, Christians bury their dead in the sure and certain promise of the resurrection of the body. This is the purpose of the rite of **Committal**.

FUNERAL SERVICE

THE ORDER OF SERVICE

The funeral service is the Church's public proclamation of Christ crucified to the specific situation of the death of a Christian. Of all the burial rites, the funeral service is the chief opportunity for the deceased, or the deceased's family, to confess the hope that each Christian has for the journey through death to life.

Let us look at the funeral service commonly used in the Lutheran Church. The wording of the funeral service is located on the left side of the page; a brief commentary is on the right. It is good to familiarize yourself with this service so you can understand what will happen and can ask your pastor about any sections that may not be clear to you.

A hymn or psalm may be sung or spoken.

Stand

INVOCATION

The sign of the cross ✜ may be made by all in remembrance of their Baptism.

P In the name of the Father and of the ✜ Son and of the Holy Spirit.

C **Amen.**   *Matthew 28:19b*

REMEMBRANCE OF BAPTISM

The casket may be covered with a funeral pall.

P In Holy Baptism __name__ was clothed with the robe of Christ's righteousness that covered all __his/her__ sin. St. Paul says: "Do you not know that all of us who have been baptized into Christ Jesus were baptized into His death?"

C **We were buried therefore with Him by baptism into death, in order that, just as Christ was raised from the dead by the glory of the Father, we too might walk in newness of life. For if we have been united with Him in a death like His, we shall certainly be united with Him in a resurrection like His.**

Romans 6:3–5

THE INVOCATION

Those gathered in the name of Jesus have this comforting promise: "For where two or three are gathered in My name, there am I among them" (Matthew 18:20).

In this triune invocation, first spoken over us in our Baptism, we call upon the Father, Son, and Holy Spirit to bless the funeral service that follows. By this invocation, we acknowledge that we are God's redeemed children in God's house preparing to receive His good gifts to His glory. Gathered then, according to God's will, we are assured that the Lord is with us in our worship and that when we speak, God listens (Matthew 18:19–20; 28:19–20). The invocation also announces that the funeral service is done "in the name of," that is, by the authority of, the Holy Trinity. The funeral service is part of the public ministry of the Church.

REMEMBRANCE OF BAPTISM

In our Baptism, our sins are forgiven and our death is overcome. The promises that the Lord gave us in our Baptism are what give us great comfort and peace in the face of death. From beginning to end, the funeral liturgy is full of baptismal images, language, and Scripture texts. Why such an emphasis on Baptism? It is in this Sacrament that the Lord forgives our sin, covers our shame, takes away the sting of death, and dispels the darkness of the grave.

On the cross, Jesus dies in our place; His blood quenches the wrath of God that we deserve.

The water and Word of Holy Baptism deliver this promise of forgiveness and the good pleasure of our heavenly Father to us. In Baptism, we are declared to be children of our heavenly Father, with Jesus as our brother and heaven our sure inheritance.

The comfort of Baptism is offered in this part of the funeral service with the reading of Romans 6:3–5 and the covering of the casket with the funeral pall. The pastor may begin the service at the back of the church, where the text is read responsively as the casket is draped with the funeral pall.

The white funeral pall is a visual representation of the righteousness that Jesus imputes to His people. Like a baby dressed in a white baptismal gown, the white pall is a picture of the holiness in which the Lord has clothed His saints. In his vision of the heavenly sanctuary, St. John sees the saints in heaven clothed in white robes. "These are the ones coming out of the great tribulation. They have washed their robes and made them white in the blood of the Lamb" (Revelation 7:14). As we cover the casket with the pall, we rejoice that the Lord Jesus has clothed our beloved dead in the eternal splendor of His death-won righteousness.

Another visual connection to Baptism may be made through the use of the paschal candle. When used, the paschal candle is lit before the beginning of the service and placed in the chancel to be near the head of the casket as a sign of the hope of the resurrection into which the deceased was baptized.

INTROIT, PSALM, OR ENTRANCE HYMN

INTROIT, PSALM, or
ENTRANCE HYMN

In the shadow of the grave, the Lord's people sing hymns and psalms of life. The Psalter has been the Church's songbook for centuries. A favorite psalm, either complete or in part, can express the depth of feelings that death stirs in the bereaved. A psalm can also beautifully confess the faith we have in our loving and gracious Savior.

There is also the option to use a hymn during the entrance of the casket and family into the church. Martin Luther encourages us to sing hymns of heaven and the resurrection:

Nor do we sing any dirges or doleful songs over our dead and at the grave, but comforting hymns of the forgiveness of sins, of rest, sleep, life, and of the resurrection of departed Christians so that our faith may be strengthened and the people be moved to true devotion.

In a wonderful way, our songs and hymns are a mockery of death, a refusal to believe its lie that it is the end. Rather, we sing that there is life on the other side of death, life with my Jesus who lives and reigns to all eternity. Our singing declares the Lord's triumph over sin, death, and the devil. (See p. 54 for a list of suggested hymns.)

During the singing of the entrance hymn, the pastor leads the casket and the bereaved into the church. It is appropriate that the procession be led with a processional cross. "The use of a processional cross indicates that Christ not only leads the church in life, but also leads the Christian through death to eternal life."

KYRIE

In life and in death, we are totally dependent on the Lord's mercy and grace, totally dependent on His gifts. Oftentimes, the funerals of non-Christians focus on the person's life and works. The funeral of a Christian focuses instead on the death of Jesus and His merciful gifts to us. Trusting in His mercy, we pray, "Lord, have mercy upon us. Christ, have mercy upon us. Lord, have mercy upon us."

KYRIE ~ *Lord, Have Mercy*

Mark 10:47

P Lord, have mercy upon us.
C **Christ, have mercy upon us.
Lord, have mercy upon us.**

SALUTATION and COLLECT OF THE DAY

P The Lord be with you.   *2 Timothy 4:22*
C **And also with you.**

P Let us pray.
O God of grace and mercy, we give thanks
for Your loving-kindness shown to
___name___ and to all Your servants who,
having finished their course in faith,
now rest from their labors. Grant that we
also may be faithful unto death and receive
the crown of eternal life; through Jesus
Christ, Your Son, our Lord, who lives and
reigns with You and the Holy Spirit, one
God, now and forever. (546)
C **Amen.**
Sit

OLD TESTAMENT or FIRST READING

After the reading:

A This is the Word of the Lord.
C **Thanks be to God.**

PSALM or GRADUAL

EPISTLE or SECOND READING

After the reading:

A This is the Word of the Lord.
C **Thanks be to God.**

Stand

VERSE

General
A Alleluia, alle- | luia.*
Jesus Christ is the firstborn | of the dead;
C **to Him be glory and power
for- | ever.***
Alle- | luia.   *[Revelation 1:5–6]*

Lent
A If we have | died with Christ,*
we shall also | live with Him;
C **if we are faithful | to the end,***
we shall | reign with Him.
2 Timothy 2:11b–12a

SALUTATION AND COLLECT OF THE DAY

The Collect gives thanks to God for His gifts given to our beloved departed in his or her life and death. It asks the Lord to mercifully keep us in the same gifts and bring us also to the blessings of eternal life.

This prayer gives two wonderful names to eternal life: *rest* and *crowns*. Heaven is a rest because the constant struggles of this world are finally ended; our battles against the flesh and the devil are over. In heaven, we rest in the peace won through Jesus' cross.

The "crown" of life is the other beautiful name given to heaven. Life, eternal life, is the splendor of the Lord's people. We can say with confidence, "Those who fall asleep in the Lord are not dead, but are finally alive, crowned with life."

SCRIPTURE READINGS

While faithful departed have the comfort of seeing the Lord's face and hearing the songs of the angels, those who are left behind find comfort in His Word (Romans 15:4). In His Word, we hear that death is not the end. In His Word, we hear that all of our sins and death and deserved wrath were piled on His back and that He suffered and died in our place. In His Word, we behold the Lamb of God who takes away the sin of the world. In His Word, we hear these promises for us: that we are baptized, forgiven, and loved by God our Father and His Son, our Lord Jesus. Through His Word echo the promises of our great hope, the resurrection of the body and the life everlasting.

HOLY GOSPEL

P The Holy Gospel according to St.
_____, the _____ chapter.
C **Glory to You, O Lord.**

After the reading:

P This is the Gospel of the Lord.
C **Praise to You, O Christ.**

APOSTLES' CREED

P God has made us His people through our
Baptism into Christ. Living together in
trust and hope, we confess our faith.
C **I believe in God, the Father Almighty,**
maker of heaven and earth.

And in Jesus Christ, His only Son,
our Lord,
who was conceived by the
Holy Spirit,
born of the virgin Mary,
suffered under Pontius Pilate,
was crucified, died and was buried.
He descended into hell.
The third day He rose again from
the dead.
He ascended into heaven
and sits at the right hand of God
the Father Almighty.
From thence He will come to judge
the living and the dead.
I believe in the Holy Spirit,
the holy Christian Church,
the communion of saints,
the forgiveness of sins,
the resurrection of the body,
and the life ✝ everlasting. Amen.

Christian: the ancient text reads "catholic," meaning the whole
Church as it confesses the wholeness of Christian doctrine.

Sit

The Holy Spirit, who called all believers to faith, gathers them to hear the Word of God. The Christian is sustained by the Lord's Word that gives the Lord's promised life (Matthew 4:4). In His Word, the bereaved Christian finds comfort and life and peace.

The pastor, often in consultation with the family, will choose the texts to be read in the service. It is acceptable to use texts appointed for the previous Sunday, confirmation verses, or other favorite passages. In the context of the funeral service, special care should be taken to select Scripture texts that emphasize the forgiveness of sin, the sure hope in the resurrection of the dead, and life everlasting. (A list of suggested Scripture texts is available on p. 52.)

APOSTLES' CREED

As we publicly confess the faith that we have received, we hear what the Holy Trinity has done for us. *God the Father* has created all creatures and us, and He has given us life and all that we need to support it.

God the Son, our Lord Jesus, has redeemed us with His holy, precious blood and His innocent suffering and death. His crucifixion and death strip the sting out of death, and His resurrection gives us the sure hope of our own resurrection to eternal life.

God the Holy Spirit has brought to us the promise of the Gospel. By His gift of faith, He has numbered us with the redeemed, forgiven us, and through Baptism has made us members of the Holy Christian Church. In His Church, we are kept safe and strengthened against the attacks of sin and the devil. On the Last Day, the Holy Spirit will raise all the dead and us and give eternal life to all believers in Jesus.

Here in the funeral service, the confession "I believe in the forgiveness of sins, the resurrection of the body, and the life everlasting" sounds forth with the robust confidence of faith.

HYMN OF THE DAY

The hymn of the day is the principle hymn of the funeral service and relates to the theme of the day from the Holy Gospel. Hymns enable everyone to join together in proclaiming the scriptural truths read at the lectern, preached from the pulpit, and spoken before the altar. In the hymns, we respond to this Good News with singing, reciting back to God the great acts of our salvation in thanksgiving and praise. (A list of suggested hymns is available on p. 54.)

SERMON

While a pastor will take care to address the specific concerns of the mourning family, friends, and congregation, there are two essential elements that are common to all Lutheran sermons: Law and Gospel.

In a funeral, the Law has often done its work before a word is ever preached from the pulpit. The Lord speaks to us in His Law, which shows us His righteousness and our sin. The Law is meant to humble the proud and arrogant and show them their need for a Savior. We know that death is not good, that creation was not meant to be like this. When a loved one dies, we are reminded again of our own mortality. We are brought up short with the realization that we, too, will one day breathe our last breath. It simply remains for the sermon to show the root cause of the tragedy of death: sin. "The wages of sin is death" (Romans 6:23).

Then the Gospel, which gives us the Lord's righteousness and the forgiveness of sins, sweeps in and drives out despair and sorrow. The Gospel is meant to lift up the humble and despairing with the certainty that our sins are forgiven. Our Lord Jesus Christ defeated death,

| HYMN OF THE DAY |
| SERMON |

destroyed the devil, and won the forgiveness of all sin through His death on the cross and His resurrection from the grave.

In the funeral sermon, we hear that God has given this victory over death to our loved ones both in their life and now in their death. We hear that the deceased even now stand before the Lord's face in glory and know the fullness of joy that is His presence. We hear that their suffering is over, that their battle against the devil, the world, and their sinful nature is finished, and that they now know perfect peace.

Unlike a eulogy, which focuses on the past, a Christian funeral sermon focuses on the present and the future. The faithful departed rejoiced in the Lord's grace in their lives, they rejoice even more now as they enjoy the presence of Christ, and their joy will be complete on the great day of the resurrection of all flesh.

Unlike a eulogy, which is about the good works of the departed, the Christian funeral sermon is about the works, life, and death of Jesus. It is faith that fights back despair, and faith comes from hearing the Word of Christ (Romans 10:17).

The funeral sermon, like every Christian sermon, proclaims the Good News of Jesus and His goodness for us. As we walk through this vale of tears, we have the confidence that Jesus does not leave us as orphans but comes to us with His comforting promises. We rejoice in His goodness to our beloved dead, and we rejoice in His goodness to us as well. The funeral sermon gives these Gospel promises to all who hear it, and by faith in these promises, our hearts are sure that we, too, will reach the place that Jesus has prepared for us (John 14:1–4).

Finally, the funeral sermon directs the hearts and minds of the mourners to the Christian's great hope: the return of Jesus, the resurrection of the body, and the life everlasting. The funeral service is the halfway point between our Baptism and our resurrection. We "plant" our dead in the ground in the sure hope that they will rise up on the Last Day, having passed through death to life everlasting (1 Corinthians 15:35–49).

Kneel/Stand

PRAYER OF THE CHURCH [1 Timothy 2:1–4]

P   Let us pray to the Lord, our God and
Father, who raised Jesus from the dead.

After each portion of the prayers:

P   Lord, in Your mercy,

C   **hear our prayer.**

The prayers conclude:

C   **Amen.**

*When there is Holy Communion, the service continues
with the OFFERTORY in the Divine Service; otherwise, the
service continues with the LORD'S PRAYER.*

LORD'S PRAYER Matthew 6:9–13

P   Taught by our Lord and trusting His
promises, we are bold to pray:

C   **Our Father who art in heaven,
     hallowed be Thy name,
     Thy kingdom come,
     Thy will be done on earth as it is
       in heaven;
     give us this day our daily bread;
     and forgive us our trespasses as we
       forgive those who trespass
       against us;
     and lead us not into temptation,
     but deliver us from evil.
   For Thine is the kingdom and the power
     and the glory forever and ever. Amen.**

*Following the LORD'S PRAYER (or the DISTRIBUTION when
there is Holy Communion), the pastor takes his place
at the casket.*

PRAYER OF THE CHURCH AND THE LORD'S PRAYER

The Christian life is one of prayer. We take comfort in the Lord's promise to hear and answer our prayers: "Call upon Me in the day of trouble; I will deliver you, and you shall glorify Me" (Psalm 50:15). The prayers of the funeral liturgy include petitions for the Church in heaven and on earth to know the Lord's peace, thanksgiving for the gifts of life given to our beloved dead, and a prayer that by the Lord's mercy we would know His comfort and peace. We pray for the resurrection, for the soon return of Jesus, for the spread of His Word of life in this world of death, for comfort for those who mourn, and for the faith that clings to Jesus and His promises in this life of trouble and tears. We pray with the confidence that nothing can separate us from God's love for us in Christ, knowing that at last we, too, will be brought to our heavenly home to see the Lord face-to-face and to know the eternal joys of paradise.

The prayers end with the congregation joining together in the Lord's Prayer. The Lord's Prayer is the chief prayer of the Christian Church, and here in the funeral service we are reminded of the all-encompassing grace of God, who provides all that we need for this body and life. The congregation prays, "Thy kingdom come," and reflects upon the message heard in the readings, hymns, and sermon of the sure and certain hope of the Last Day. We pray, "Thy will be done," and encounter again the reality present before us that God's will for our lives is not always known (Isaiah 55:7–9). We pray for forgiveness of sins and hear Christ's own Word proclaiming that in His death He has accomplished everything needed to "forgive our trespasses."

NUNC DIMITTIS ~ THE SONG OF SIMEON

The Nunc Dimittis is surrounded by the marvelous promise of Jesus: "I am the resurrection and the life. Whoever believes in Me, though he die, yet shall he live, and everyone who lives and believes in Me shall never die" (John 11:25–26). These are the words our Lord spoke to Martha as she mourned the death of her brother, Lazarus. For Martha and for us, this promise delivers the sweetest comfort. Because our Jesus is the resurrection and the life, we know that He will bring us through death to His eternal life.

We then speak or sing the Nunc Dimittis. This hymn is familiar; it is sung every Sunday as the Lord's people leave the altar after eating and drinking the body and blood of the Lord. The Nunc Dimittis was originally sung in the temple when the old and faithful Israelite Simeon took the baby Jesus into his arms (Luke 2:25–35). Looking at the face of Jesus, Simeon gave thanks to God for being allowed to see the Messiah before he died. He held in his arms the Peace of the whole world. Now we sing with Simeon. We have heard of the Lord Jesus, of His cross and death and resurrection. We know the peace that He has made between man and God in the forgiveness of our sins. We have tasted the Lord's

---

NUNC DIMITTIS ~ *Song of Simeon*

A "I am the resurrection and the life," says the Lord. "He who believes in Me will live, even though he dies; and whoever lives and believes in Me will never die."

John 11:25–26 NIV

C **Lord, now You let Your servant go in peace;**
Your word has been fulfilled.
My own eyes have seen the salvation
which You have prepared in the sight of every people:
a light to reveal You to the nations
and the glory of Your people Israel.

Luke 2:29–32

Glory be to the Father and to the Son and to the Holy Spirit;
as it was in the beginning, is now, and will be forever. Amen.

A "I am the resurrection and the life," says the Lord. "He who believes in Me will live, even though he dies; and whoever lives and believes in Me will never die."

---

goodness and believed His promises. Having been prepared by God, we, like Simeon, are ready for death and the blessings of eternal life with our Jesus.

CONCLUDING COLLECT

We have received God's good gifts in the Word. However, before we continue to committing the body of our dead loved one to the ground, we pause to thank the Lord Jesus for all that He has done for us.

The concluding collect "collects" our grateful thoughts into one short prayer thanking the Good Shepherd for bringing our beloved dead to their eternal home and again asking that He would graciously bring us to the joyful reunion of the faithful.

BENEDICAMUS AND BENEDICTION

We bless the Lord because He has blessed us and been merciful to us.

We end the funeral service as we began—in the name of the Lord and with a threefold speaking of God's holy name. As we mourn death, we might wonder if the Lord loves us or hates us if He frowns at us or smiles upon us. In the Benediction, we hear that the Holy Trinity smiles upon us. His smile, His promise, and His gracious care and love for us give us peace, even in the sorrow of death. We depart to take up the next task in peace and with God's blessing.

CONCLUDING COLLECT

P The Lord be with you. *2 Timothy 4:22*
C **And also with you.**

P Let us pray.
Lord God, our shepherd, You gather the lambs of Your flock into the arms of Your mercy and bring them home. Comfort us with the certain hope of the resurrection to everlasting life and a joyful reunion with those we love who have died in the faith; through Jesus Christ, Your Son, our Lord, who lives and reigns with You and the Holy Spirit, one God, now and forever.
(549)
C **Amen.**

BENEDICAMUS and BENEDICTION

A Let us bless the Lord. *[Psalm 103:1]*
C **Thanks be to God.**

P The Lord bless you and keep you.
The Lord make His face shine upon you and be gracious unto you.
The Lord lift up His countenance upon you and ⊹ give you peace.
C **Amen.** *Numbers 6:24–26*

P Let us go forth in peace,
C **in the name of the Lord. Amen.**

A hymn may be sung as the casket is led in procession out of the church.

We mourn in peace. We mix our tears with hope, for there is only one thing in the world that is stronger than death: our Jesus. We have Him and He has us, and so we live in the sure promises of our Baptism, we live in the confidence of faith, and we live in His death and resurrection for us—the certain hope of the resurrection of the body and the life everlasting.

During a hymn, the casket is led in procession out of the church. Before the procession leaves the church, the pall is removed and left in the church. The procession then makes its way to the place of interment. The funeral service continues at the site of the burial or interment with the committal service. Much that has been heard in the church is echoed at the committal service as the comfort of the Lord's death and resurrection are brought all the way to the grave.

COMMITTAL

The Committal is used for internment in a place previously set apart for burial. In the case of cremation, the ashes are buried or interred at a cemetary plot, mausoleum, crypt, or columbarium. The practice of scattering the ashes of the deceased to the elements is discouraged among Christians. When circumstances require the burial occur at a later date, the Committal may include a sermon following the Scripture reading(s).

PROCESSIONAL SCRIPTURES

The procession continues at the cemetery, with the processional cross (if possible) and the pastor leading the casket to the grave. During the procession, the pastor reads various Scriptures of mourning and hope. It is by the Word of God that the Holy Spirit creates and sustains faith in the Lord's promises. It is especially stunning to be surrounded by tombstones and graves while hearing the promises of the resurrection. These are the graves that will open when Jesus returns and calls out the dead.

COLLECT

If the interment is in a public cemetery, the collect for the blessing of a grave is used. This prayer speaks of the Lord's three-day rest in the tomb and His resurrection and asks that the Lord would keep this grave in peace until the resurrection of the dead.

If the committal is in a church cemetery, the opening prayer gives thanks to God for the blessings given to the faithful, including the hope of the resurrection.

SCRIPTURE READINGS

The Scriptures appointed for the committal beautifully extol the promise of the resurrection. The body that we plant in the ground is the same one that the Lord will call forth on the Last Day. The Scriptures suggested are John 12:23–26; 1 Corinthians 15:42–49; 1 Corinthians 15:51–57; and 1 Thessalonians 4:13–17.

If the grave is to be blessed:

P Let us pray.
O Lord Jesus Christ, by Your three-day rest in the tomb You hallowed the graves of all who believe in You, promising resurrection to our mortal bodies. Bless ☩ this grave that the body of our _brother/sister_ may sleep here in peace until You awaken _him/her_ to glory, when _he/she_ will see You face to face and know the splendor of the eternal God, for You live and reign with the Father and the Holy Spirit, one God, now and forever. (551)

C **Amen.**

If the grave has already been blessed:

P Let us pray.
Merciful Father and Lord of life, with whom live the spirits of those who depart in the faith, we thank You for the blessings of body and soul that You granted this departed _brother/sister_, whose earthly remains we now lay to rest. Above all, we rejoice at Your gracious promise to all Your servants, both living and departed, that we shall be raised from death at the coming of our Lord Jesus Christ, who lives and reigns with You and the Holy Spirit, one God, now and forever. (552)

THE COMMITTAL

The committal is taken from Genesis 3:19 and Philippians 3:21. This wonderful combination of texts moves from the curse to the resurrection. Because of our sin, we go back to the earth, but because of Jesus' resurrection, we will only be dust and ashes for a little while. At the Lord's return, we will be like Him in His glorious body.

When the Committal does not immediately follow the Funeral Service, the CREED may be confessed.

P God has made us His people through our Baptism into Christ. Living together in trust and hope, we confess our faith.

C **I believe in God, the Father Almighty,**
    maker of heaven and earth.
And in Jesus Christ, His only Son, our Lord,
    who was conceived by the Holy Spirit,
    born of the virgin Mary,
    suffered under Pontius Pilate,
    was crucified, died and was buried.
    He descended into hell.
    The third day He rose again from the dead.
    He ascended into heaven
    and sits at the right hand of God the Father Almighty.
    From thence He will come to judge the living and the dead.
I believe in the Holy Spirit,
    the holy Christian Church,
        the communion of saints,
    the forgiveness of sins,
    the resurrection of the body,
    and the life ✠ everlasting. Amen.

Christian: the ancient text reads "catholic," meaning the whole Church as it confesses the wholeness of Christian doctrine.

Sand or earth may be poured on the casket in the sign of the cross while the pastor says:

P We now commit the body of our _brother/sister_ _name_ to _the ground / its resting place / the deep_ ; earth to earth, ashes to ashes, dust to dust, in the sure and certain hope of the resurrection to eternal life through our Lord Jesus Christ, who will change our lowly bodies so that they will be like His glorious body, by the power that enables Him to subdue all things to Himself.

The pastor may place his hand on the head of the casket as he says:

P May God the Father, who created this body; may God the ✠ Son, who by His blood redeemed this body; may God the Holy Spirit, who by Holy Baptism sanctified this body to be His temple, keep these remains to the day of the resurrection of all flesh.

C Amen.

P Taught by our Lord and trusting His promises, we are bold to pray:

C Our Father who art in heaven,
hallowed be Thy name,
Thy kingdom come,
Thy will be done on earth as it is in heaven;
give us this day our daily bread;
and forgive us our trespasses
as we forgive those who trespass against us;
and lead us not into temptation,
but deliver us from evil.
For Thine is the kingdom and the power and the glory
forever and ever. Amen.

Matthew 6:9–13

P Almighty God, by the death of Your Son Jesus Christ You destroyed death, by His rest in the tomb You sanctified the graves of Your saints, and by His bodily resurrection You brought life and immortality to light so that all who die in Him abide in peace and hope. Receive our thanks for the victory over death and the grave that He won for us. Keep us in everlasting communion with all who wait for Him on earth and with all in heaven who are with Him, for He is the resurrection and the life, even Jesus Christ, our Lord. (550)

C Amen.

THE BLESSING OF THE BODY

Because of the coming resurrection, Christian respect is shown toward the body even to the very end. In fact, the laying of the body in the grave also shows this respect. The Holy Trinity has had dealings with this body in creation, redemption, and sanctification, and the resurrection will bring this very body back to life.

LORD'S PRAYER AND CONCLUDING PRAYER

The Lord's Prayer is prayed, along with a prayer thanking the Lord Jesus for His victory over the grave. This prayer is especially poignant prayed at the face of an open grave. The grave before us is opened to receive the body of our loved one, but because Jesus walked out of the tomb, this grave will also be opened on the Last Day to give this dear saint new life.

The following or another appropriate hymn may be sung.

Abide with me, fast falls the eventide.
The darkness deepens; Lord, with me abide.
When other helpers fail and comforts flee,
Help of the helpless, O abide with me.

Hold Thou Thy cross before my closing eyes;
Shine through the gloom, and point me to the skies.
Heav'n's morning breaks, and earth's vain shadows flee;
In life, in death, O Lord, abide with me.   *Hymn 878:1, 6*

The conclusion of the service includes a hymn. "Abide with Me," stanzas one and six, are recommended in the *Agenda*. This hymn is a prayer for the Lord's abiding presence and promises. It is only with the Lord by our side that we can pass safely through this valley of sorrow.

P Alleluia! Christ is risen.
C **He is risen indeed. Alleluia!**
P Let us go forth in peace, in the name of the Lord.
C **Amen.**

The final word in the committal service is one of victory. The Easter greeting of the Church sends away any last doubts and uncertainties. Jesus is the victor over the grave, the conqueror of death, and His conquering victory was for us. The grave seems strong, but the love of Jesus for us is stronger and undying.

P The Lord bless you and keep you.
The Lord make His face shine upon you and be gracious unto you.
The Lord lift up His countenance upon you and ☩ give you peace.
C **Amen.**

Numbers 6:24–26

We are sent from the cemetery in peace. We will be back. We may be back to mourn the loss of another loved one, or it might be our turn to be buried. But we will return in the same peace in which we left, in the peace of our heavenly Father, who through the death of His Son has made the way for us to eternal life. Through His word of comfort and promise, He has given us the assurance that the resurrection of the body and life everlasting are our sure and unwavering hope in this life of tears.

FOR THE LIVING AND THE DEAD

There is one last thing to say about Christian burial. It is often heard: "The funeral service is for the living, not the dead." Certainly the service is for the living, but why leave out the dead? The living hear the Word of God and are comforted in their sorrow, but the act of Christian burial is for the dead. It is a gift of love that the family and the Shurch is giving to the one who has died.

Have you ever watched a loving mother lay her sleeping child in bed? There is such care and tenderness in her actions. She carries him carefully to the bed, tucks him in, and kisses his forehead. The child knows nothing of it; he is asleep. But the mother loves the child and takes care of him, whether he is sleeping or awake. The funeral of a Christian is a very similar event. With loving care, we tuck our beloved in for a long sleep, to rest until the resurrection.

We confess the resurrection of the body. Therefore, the care that Christian families and the Christian Church give to the bodies of our dead matters. Remember the women who carefully wrapped Jesus in grave clothes and laid Him in the tomb, the same women who were coming back Easter morning to anoint His body with spices. These faithful women were caring for Jesus, even after He was dead. The concern we show for the bodies of our loved ones is a confession of the resurrection: "God is not through with this body."

The funeral service is for both the living and the dead. We care for the body of our dead family member or friend, while at the same time, our heavenly Father cares for us with the comfort and peace of the death of Jesus.

CONSIDER

What parts of the funeral service bring comfort to the bereaved?

How can the choice of Scripture texts and hymns support the faith of the bereaved?

How does knowing the difference between a sermon and a eulogy help you prepare for the funeral?

Many people feel uncomfortable or scared of cemeteries. How does understanding the committal service help you get past your fears?

GRIEF: WHAT TO EXPECT

But we do not want you to be uninformed, brothers, about those who are asleep, that you may not grieve as others do who have no hope. *1 Thessalonians 4:13*

The word *hope* has been prominently used in this book, and it is important to note the word's biblical usage as opposed to our worldly usage. When we say, "I hope it rains," we indicate that we do not know if it will, and even though we assume it will not, we would like it to rain. There is an embedded uncertainty when we use the word *hope*.

The opposite is true in the Scriptures. In the Bible, hope is not something uncertain or unsure. Because what we hope will come to pass is promised by God, and because God never lies, our hope is sure and certain. Hope, in the Bible, is faith directed toward the future. So when we speak of the *hope of the resurrection*, we are not saying, "I'm not sure if there will be a resurrection, but it would be nice if there were." No. In the Scriptures, hope (like faith) is casting all doubt aside. We are then saying, "God has promised to raise me and all flesh from death and give to me and all believers in Him eternal life. So I yearn and pray and eagerly expect the resurrection of the body and the life everlasting."

As Christians, we know that there is nothing wrong or sinful about grief. The Gospel sets us free to mourn and be sad at the death of our loved one. But we also rejoice that the Lord Jesus has overcome death, and He is with us in our grief. Death and sorrow cannot overcome Him, and so they cannot overcome us. The verse that speaks most clearly to the mourning Christian is 1 Thessalonians 4:13: "But we do not want you to be uninformed, brothers, about those who are asleep, that you may not grieve as others do who have no hope." We grieve, we mourn, but this is not without hope. We cry and laugh; we weep and smile; we are sad and we trust in the Lord.

Psalm 23:4 offers a wonderful road map as we travel the road of grief:

Even though I walk through the valley of the shadow of death, I will fear no evil, for You are with me; Your rod and Your staff, they comfort me.

We take comfort in the assurance that the Lord is with us. We do not grieve alone. And we take comfort in the knowledge that though the way seems dark and death seems very close, Jesus is on the path with us to care for us. There is no place for fear with the Lord at our side. Finally, we know that we are passing through the valley. We are not here to stay. The darkness of grief will give way to the joy of Jesus' gift of forgiveness and life.

Grief brings with it different waves of emotions. Each person grieves differently, but there are some emotions that we might expect, and the hope we have in our Good Shepherd, Jesus, offers us comfort in the midst of these struggles.

EXPECT SHOCK . . . *and Acceptance*

The news of a loved one's death is jarring, disorienting. "How can this be? This can't be true." In a moment, everything changes. The truth is sometimes too difficult to accept. It takes time for the reality of death to settle in.

The funeral service is an important part of this process of acceptance. In the funeral, the reality of death is matched with the reality of Jesus' death. No matter how much we are tossed around by our emotions, the love of Jesus is always secure.

It is often helpful for those who are mourning to tell the story of the death of loved ones. This helps them grasp what has happened and place this death in the context of life. A listening ear is a true gift, and it is a wonderful privilege to be entrusted with these stories.

EXPECT SADNESS . . . *and Joy*

Death is sad. Funerals are sad. Empty homes and estate sales and holidays without our loved ones are sad. There is a lingering sorrow that follows death, which we call mourning.

Jesus Himself knows what it is like to be sad. Jesus mourned the death of Lazarus. The shortest verse in the Bible concerns this very thing: "Jesus wept" (John 11:35). Jesus cried because He was sad.

The fact that Jesus, the Son of God Himself, knows the deep sadness that death causes gives us peace in the midst of tears. "If Jesus cries, it must be okay for me to cry also." Yes, cry. Death is sad. At the same time, we rejoice because the Lord's Word comforts us in sadness: Jesus has overcome death and come out of the grave. He died for us and promises us His love and eternal life.

The devil would use our sadness to push us into a debilitating darkness, a deep sadness that threatens to choke out our faith and love. This is mourning without hope. Sometimes this deep sadness can lead to a physical sickness that needs doctors and medication to address. Other times it is a spiritual condition that needs a constant diet of the Lord's Gospel. Many times it is a combination of these two. Family members and your pastor can help gauge if your sadness is dangerous to your health.

EXPECT ANGER, FRUSTRATION . . . *and Trust*

Death often causes us to question God, especially when death is sudden or tragic. "Why, God? Why her? Why now?" We even question God's love for us: "If you loved him, surely You wouldn't have let that happen? How can You love me and still let me hurt so much?" In the agony of death and the pain of suffering, God seems far away, like He's angry or does not care.

We do not know why the Lord gives out death the way He does. We do not know why this person suffers so much while that person does not. The Lord has not told us. The danger here is this: we try to figure out how the Lord feels about us based on the circumstances of our life. "If things are going well, then God must love me." Then the opposite would be true: "If things are rotten, God must hate me." But the Lord has not given us the circumstances of our life as the thermometer of His love. For this He has given the cross.

There is absolute certainty for the grieving that God loves them: Jesus died. This is the final verdict of the Lord's feelings for us, of His love.

For I am sure that neither death nor life, nor angels nor rulers, nor things present nor things to come, nor powers, nor height nor depth, nor anything else in all creation, will be able to separate us from the love of God in Christ Jesus our Lord. (Romans 8:38–39)

We might not know why God has given out this or that suffering, but we trust that He loves us, died for us, and has us as His own dear children.

EXPECT REGRET . . . *and Forgiveness*

After the death of a loved one, our consciences are often troubled with regret. There are things we wish we would have done and said and things we wish we would not have done or said. Often we sinned against our loved ones—that is what sinners do.

We are prone to make excuses and attempt to ease the pain of our guilt, but this cannot undo what has been done. Beware of excusing sin. The Gospel never excuses sin. The Gospel forgives sin. The sins that we commit against our family and friends are sins for which Jesus died. His blood covers them all. We are forgiven.

EXPECT LONELINESS . . . *and Comfort*

Death brings feelings of emptiness. The days and weeks following the death of a loved one are hectic, but eventually relatives return to their homes, friends go back to their routines, and mourners are left alone. Holidays, anniversaries, and birthdays are also times of loneliness.

The Lord has comfort for the lonely. He has promised His abiding presence: "You are with me" (Psalm 23:4). "I will never leave you nor forsake you" (Hebrews 13:5). "And behold, I am with you always, to the end of the age" (Matthew 28:20).

The Lord also gives us fellow Christians. The fellowship of the Church is a wonderful consolation to the lonely. The Holy Spirit gathers us to His Word and Sacraments with other believers. These are able to offer friendship and love, as we "bear one another's burdens" (Galatians 6:2).

Finally, we have the promise that we will see our loved ones again (see 1 Thessalonians 4:15–16). They are with Jesus now; we will be with Him soon.

The best is yet to come. The Scriptures always hold before us the sure and certain hope of the resurrection of the body and the life everlasting. On the Last Day, the Lord will bring an end to death and wipe away all our tears (see Revelation 7:17; 21:4; Isaiah 25:8; 30:19; 35:10). There is a time coming soon when mourning and crying will cease, when death itself will come to an end, when joy will have no interruption. Our tear-filled eyes stay fixed on the cross of our Lord, and our hearts yearn for that great day. "Come, Lord Jesus."

CONSIDER

How would the grief of a Christian be different from that of a non-Christian?

Do you think grief has a time limit?

What emotions come with grief? What Scriptures offer us comfort in our grief?

QUESTIONS AND ANSWERS

There are many questions about death and dying. This chapter discusses a few of the more common ones. Very often our questions about death and dying are best handled in conversations with our pastor or other Christian friends.

1. What about purgatory?

Roman Catholic theology teaches that there is a time of purification after death called "purgatory." The Catholic Catechism defines purgatory as follows: "All who die in God's grace and friendship, but still imperfectly purified, are indeed assured of their eternal salvation; but after death they undergo purification, so as to achieve the holiness necessary to enter the joy of heaven" (paragraph 1030).

However, Scripture tells us that on the cross the Lord suffered and died for all of our sins; He left nothing on the table, nothing for us to accomplish or do to reach perfection. His holiness comes to us completely as a gift. (See John 3:16–17.)

The Christian does not reach perfection in this life according to works, but by the faith in which the Lord imputes to the believer the perfect righteousness of Christ. "And to the one who does not work but believes in Him who justifies the ungodly, his faith is counted as righteousness, just as David also speaks of the blessing of the one to whom God counts righteousness apart from works: 'Blessed are those whose lawless deeds are forgiven, and whose sins are covered; blessed is the man against whom the Lord will not count his sin' " (Romans 4:5–8).

The completeness of Jesus' sacrifice, and the righteousness that the Lord imputes to those with faith, completely undoes the need for purgatory. For those who trust in Christ, there is no purification necessary. For those who die in unbelief, there is no purification possible: "Whoever believes in the Son has eternal life; whoever does not obey the Son shall not see life, but the wrath of God remains on him" (John 3:36, see also John 5:24).

2. What about cremation?

Cremation is becoming increasingly popular in the funeral industry and among Christians. In some states, cremation is more frequent than bodily burials. Christians often wonder about cremation. Is it sinful? Is it good? Will cremation prevent their resurrection of the body?

We will take up the last question first. We can be sure that nothing can prevent the resurrection of the body. No matter what happens to our bodies—either in this life or after we die—the Lord will, by His almighty power, resurrect the bodies of all people at His second coming. We say in the funeral liturgy, "Earth to earth, ashes to ashes, dust to dust," and if our bodies turn to dust (via burial) or to ashes (via fire), the Lord will still gather us up and remake our bodies in the resurrection of all flesh.

Should a Christian be cremated? Is it sinful? Is there anything wrong with cremation? The ancient Church frowned upon cremation because it was a pagan practice, and even today some practice it as a denial of the resurrection. However, for most people today, the motivations are quite different. First, cremation sometimes costs less than a traditional burial. Second, some worry that traditional cemeteries that must accommodate the burials of bodies with their attendant caskets and vaults are taking up too much room. Third, in the minds of some, the oven seems a cleaner more efficient means to return a body to the elements.

How the body is treated after death is a matter of Christian freedom. Unless a person is, by cremation, denying the resurrection of the flesh, there is no sin in cremation. The strong bias of the Scriptures and the history of the Church prefer bodily Christian burial. When we make arrangements for our body after death, we want to ask the question, "How do I best confess my faith in Jesus, His return, the resurrection of the body, and life everlasting?" According to the Scriptures, burial is such a confession (see 1 Corinthians 15:42–44).

Finally, the practice of scattering the ashes of the deceased to the elements is discouraged among Christians. It is preferable to inter the cremated remains in a cemetery or at another place set aside for such a purpose.

3. Will we recognize our loved ones in heaven?

Most certainly yes.

In the Scriptures, we see this in the story of Lazarus and the rich man (Luke 16:19–31). In the afterlife, Lazarus is Lazarus, the rich man is the same fellow (though he is now poor), and Abraham is Abraham. We also remember the Mount of Transfiguration, where Jesus talks with Moses and Elijah (Luke 9:28–36). Peter and the other three apostles recognize the prophets.

It seems like many people imagine our heavenly existence as a faceless blob with no personality. This is not true. When we are in heaven, and especially after the Lord's return and the resurrection, we will be set free from sin and death, but not from our personalities, not from our name. We are the same people who are born, baptized, cared for by Jesus, and brought from this valley of death to the Lord's eternal kingdom. Far from not knowing our friends and loved ones, in heaven we will finally know and be known.

4. What about reincarnation?

Many Eastern religions and some esoteric religions in the West teach reincarnation, that a part of the person (soul or spirit) passes, after death, into another body. This teaching is completely foreign to the Scriptures. "And just as it is appointed for man to die once, and after that comes judgment, so Christ, having been offered once to bear the sins of many, will appear a second time, not to deal with sin but to save those who are eagerly waiting for Him" (Hebrews 9:27–28).

5. What music is appropriate in the funeral service?

Being a worship service of the triune God, only Christian hymns should be used in the funeral service. The hymnals available in our Lutheran churches are full of hymns of comfort and the Lord's promise of life. The hymns chosen for the funeral service should proclaim the works and promises of our Lord Jesus, His death, His resurrection, His forgiveness, and His promise of everlasting life.

If a reception or meal is held after the funeral service, it may be appropriate to have music that was not used in the service. This music could be favorites or reminiscent of the deceased.

A list of music suggestions may be found on pages 54–55.

6. What about eulogies?

A eulogy is not in the best Christian tradition. An obituary may be read that focuses on the Gospel promise of salvation by grace alone through faith alone in Christ our Lord and not on the good deeds of the deceased.

It might be appropriate for family and friends to say a few words about the beloved dead in a more casual setting, such as a reception or family gathering after the service.

WHEN PLANNING A FUNERAL

Heavenly Father, Your Son promised that those who confess You before men will be confessed before You in heaven. Grant us Your Holy Spirit that we would make the good confession of Jesus through this funeral service. May all who attend it hear of Your mercy and love. May You be glorified, and may we be given Your peace. May the worship of You and Your Son and the Holy Spirit be a small foretaste of the joys of heaven, and bring all of Your people unto the eternal wedding feast of Your Son and His Church. *Amen.*

CONFESSING CHRIST WITH MY FUNERAL

[Jesus says:] "Everyone who acknowledges Me before men, I also will acknowledge before My Father who is in heaven." *Matthew 10:32*

We all know that death is coming. It is wise to arrange our affairs to make it easier on those whom we leave behind. Just as it is very important to have a will, it is also good to make arrangements for your funeral. Funeral homes have different plans you can purchase, such as coffins, services, and cemetery plots. A funeral director can help you through this process and will normally provide an extensive list of things that can be arranged before death.

In the next few pages, we will be concerned with arrangements for the funeral service itself. Our funerals are a wonderful opportunity (probably our last opportunity on this earth) to confess our faith in Christ. When planning our funeral, we are answering one question: "How might I best confess the Lord Jesus to my friends and family?"

A funeral planning worksheet is provided at the end of this book to help answer this question. Many funeral planning worksheets have a place to suggest hymns and Scripture text. This worksheet moves beyond that, including a place to make your confession of faith.

When choosing Scripture texts and hymns, people often ask, "Which one is my favorite?" This is a fine question, and it is a gift from God that we have our favorite texts and songs. When planning our funeral service, though, we want to understand this selection a bit more. Why is this my favorite? What does it say about Jesus? How does it give the promise of forgiveness, the hope of the resurrection?

May God grant that when people sing the last "Amen" of your funeral service, their ears and hearts would be full of the good gifts of our Lord Jesus.

PLANNING MY FUNERAL SERVICE

The first question to answer is this: "What would I have my funeral service confess?" Our faith in Christ, certainly. The hope founded on the resurrection, the joy of our Baptism, and the certainty of life everlasting. Consider the creeds, the catechism, the Gospels, and the death and resurrection of Jesus when you write your confession. Here are some examples:

- "I want my funeral to confess my faith in Christ and the sure hope of the resurrection of the body and the life everlasting."

- "Jesus Christ is my Lord."

- "In my Baptism, the Lord forgave my sins and has me as His own."

Just writing this confession is a wonderful gift to give to your family. Such a written confession can also serve the pastor as he confesses from the pulpit the faith of the one who has died. Remember, this is not a test. This is an opportunity to speak of your faith in Jesus to those whom you love. It is good to talk through these arrangements with your spouse, your family, your pastor, even your friends.

Flowing from this confession of faith, you may want to choose Scriptures and hymns that further express that confession. Again, do more than choose a few of your favorites. Rather, look for hymns and Scriptures that confess your faith and hold forth the gifts that the Lord gives. Jot down a few words about the hymns and Scriptures that you choose, for example:

Scripture Readings:

- *Psalm:* Psalm 27—Especially verse 4; gives the hope of the Christian, forever beholding the beauty of the Lord.

- *Old Testament:* Job 19:23–27—Job and I both know that my Redeemer, Jesus, lives.

- *Epistle:* Romans 4:5–8—I am blessed because I am justified, forgiven, accounted righteous.

- *Gospel:* John 14:1–6—If you are reading this, I am already in the place Jesus prepared for me.

Hymns:

- "Behold a Host, Arrayed in White" (*LSB* 676)—A vivid description of the Church Triumphant is given in this hymn.

- "For All the Saints" (*LSB* 677)—This hymn demonstrates that we are saints, connected to Christ our Lord and to each other.

- "Jesus Christ, My Sure Defense" (*LSB* 741)—As a clear proclamation of the hope we have in Christ, this hymn draws all Christians into this confession.

- "Lord, Thee I Love with All My Heart" (*LSB* 708)—This hymn takes us from death to the grave to the resurrection, all the way to the new heaven and the new earth.

- "Now Thank We All Our God" (*LSB* 895)—When we say good-bye, we also say thank You to the God of our salvation.

- "O Day Full of Grace" (*LSB* 503)—This is a proclamation of the Gospel of Jesus Christ, giving His life story and purpose for coming to this world.

- "O Little Flock, Fear Not the Foe" (*LSB* 666)—With Jesus on our side, there is nothing to fear: not sin, not death, not the grave, nothing.

- "Salvation unto Us Has Come" (*LSB* 555)—Luther's great Reformation hymn gives us the Law in its sternness and the Gospel in all its sweetness. This is a hymn of great comfort.

- "The Will of God Is Always Best" (*LSB* 758)—This hymn places God's will before ours.

Remember, this information is not written in stone. This is not a new law, a new form of coercion. If you come across a Scripture or a hymn that you really love, add it to the list. Change what you have written; start over if you want. There are plenty of things in this life that we are tempted to worry about. Please do not let this worksheet be one of them. It is meant simply to help you go about the joyful business of freely confessing your Jesus.

SUGGESTED READINGS
FOR THE FUNERAL SERVICE

We hear the Word of God as He presents to us readings from the Old and New Testaments. After the Old Testament reading, having a soloist or Resurrection Choir (see p. 53 for more information) present a musical setting of Psalm 23 (or another appropriate one) gives those who are grieving an opportunity to reflect on the reading just heard. In the same way, providing an appropriate verse with Alleluias prepares us to hear the Gospel of the day, just as we do on Sundays in the Divine Service.

PSALMS
23, 27, 46, 90, 91, 98, 100, 103, 116, 121, 130, 148, 156

OLD TESTAMENT
Job 19:25–26
Proverbs 3:5–6
Ecclesiastes 3:1–8 (9–15)
Isaiah 12:2–6
Isaiah 40:28–31

Isaiah 43:1–3
Isaiah 53:4–5
Jeremiah 29:11–14
Lamentations 3:22–26, 31–33

GOSPELS
Mark 10:13–17
Matthew 11:28–30
Luke 2:1–20
Luke 2:25–32

Luke 8:1–8 (9–25)

Luke 18:1–8

John 5:24–29

John 6:35–40

John 11:21–27

John 11:25–26a

John 12:23–26

John 14:1–6

John 14:25–27

EASTER STORY

Mark 16:1–8

Matthew 28:1–10

Luke 24:1–12

John 20:1–8

OTHER NEW TESTAMENT READINGS

Romans 5:1–11

Romans 5:17–21

Romans 6:3–11

Romans 8:26–29

Romans 8:31–39

Romans 14:7–8

1 Corinthians 13:1–13

1 Corinthians 15:12–26

1 Corinthians 15:51–54 (56–58)

Philippians 3:20–21

Philippians 4:4–7 (8–9)

Philippians 4:8–13

1 Thessalonians 4:13–18

1 Thessalonians 5:9

1 Timothy 3:7–8

1 Timothy 6:11–12

Hebrews 13:5–6

1 Peter 1:3–9

1 Peter 5:7–11

1 John 3:1–2

Revelation 7:13–17

Revelation 21:3–7

MUSIC RESOURCES FOR THE FUNERAL SERVICE

RESURRECTION CHOIR

In a time of grief and sorrow, finding words to say and sing may be difficult. It is at such a time that the Church, through pastors and musicians, gives us the words we are searching for. Most recognize the assistance given by the organist who leads the hymns of the funeral service. A more recent gift found in many churches is that of the Resurrection Choir, which is comprised of volunteers who are likely to have daytime availability.

The role of the Resurrection Choir is that of supporting the family with its presence and helping the family with the hymns and liturgy of hope. The choir rehearses once or twice during the year and then about forty-five minutes before the funeral. Choir members are notified by phone or e-mail and participate when their schedules permit. The repertoire of the choir is usually a setting of Psalm 23, the appropriate Verse and Alleluia, and a setting of the Nunc Dimittis. Other appropriate music may also be learned.

CONGREGATIONAL HYMNS

"Abide with Me" (*LSB* 878)
"Alleluia, Alleluia! Hearts to Heaven" (*LSB* 477)
"Behold a Host, Arrayed in White" (*LSB* 676)
"For All the Saints" (*LSB* 677)
"For Me to Live Is Jesus" (*LSB* 742)
"I Am Content! My Jesus Ever Lives" (*LSB* 468)
"I Know That My Redeemer Lives" (*LSB* 461)
"If Christ Had Not Been Raised from Death" (*LSB* 486)
"I'm But a Stranger Here" (*LSB* 748)
"In the Very Midst of Life" (*LSB* 755)
"Jesus Christ, My Sure Defense" (*LSB* 741)
"Jesus Lives! The Victory's Won" (*LSB* 490)
"Now Thank We All Our God" (*LSB* 895)
"O Day Full of Grace" (*LSB* 503)
"Oh, How Blest Are They" (*LSB* 679)
"The Will of God Is Always Best" (*LSB* 758)
"There Is a Time for Everything" (*LSB* 762)
"This Body in the Grave We Lay" (*LSB* 759)
"What God Ordains Is Always Good" (*LSB* 760)
"Why Should Cross and Trial Grieve Me" (*LSB* 756)

NUNC DIMITTIS—THE SONG OF SIMEON

Hymnic settings of the Nunc Dimittis include:

- *LSB* 937   "Lord, Bid Your Servant Go in Peace"
- *LSB* 938   "In Peace and Joy I Now Depart" (Luther's paraphrase of the Nunc Dimittis)
- *LSB*, p. 165   "Lord, Now You Let Your Servant Go in Peace"
- *LSB*, p. 199   "Lord, Now Lettest Thou Thy Servant Depart in Peace"
- *LSB*, p. 211   "O Lord, Now Let Your Servant"
- *LSB*, p. 258   "Guide Us Waking, O Lord"

From the CPH Catalog:

- 98-3733   "Lord, Now You Let Your Servant Go in Peace," Carl Schalk;
      Unison or 2-part, optional handbells, organ, optional congregation
- 98-3809   "Nunc Dimittis," Donald Busarow; SATB, organ, cantor

MUSIC FOR SOLOIST

A soloist or choir could sing any of the congregational hymns listed on page 54. If a hymn is used, perhaps a soloist could sing one of the stanzas.

The following anthems, while written for various vocal forces, provide great material for the soloist in the funeral service.

- 98-3710   "Alleluia! For Christ the Lord Is Risen," Bach/Leavitt;
      Unison, keyboard
- 98-3458   "Be Not Afraid," R. Nelson; Unison, keyboard
- 98-3193   "Behold, God Is My Salvation," Lind; Unison, keyboard
- 98-3866   "For You, O Lord, Have Delivered," Hildebrand;
      Unison, keyboard
- 98-3981   "God's Own Child, I Gladly Say It," Hildebrand;
      Unison, 2pt, keyboard
- 98-3168   "He Shall Give His Angels Charge," Busarow; Unison, organ
- 98-3733   "Lord, Now You Let Your Servant Go," Schalk;
      Unison, organ
- 98-3429   "Lord, Thee I Love with All My Heart," Busarow;
      2pt, organ, instrument
- 98-3696   "Peace I Leave with You," Kosche; 2pt, keyboard
- 98-3863   "Peace Is My Last Gift to You," Frahm; 2pt, organ

From *The Morning Star Choir Book*   97-6287
    "What God Ordains Is Always Good," Pachelbel; Unison, organ

From *A Second Morning Star Choir Book*   97-4702
    "In God, My Faithful God," Buxtehude; Unison, organ
    "If Thou But Suffer God to Guide Thee," Neumark; Unison, organ

From *A Third Morning Star Choir Book*   97-4972
    "God Is Ever Sun and Shield," Bach; Unison, organ
    "Awake, My Heart, with Gladness," Crueger; Unison, organ

PRAYERS AT THE TIME OF DEATH

FOR THE BLESSINGS OF ETERNAL LIFE

Heavenly Father, Your Son, Jesus Christ, has promised eternal life to all who believe in Him. Give to us, Your children, a sure trust in this promise, that we, too, would pass through death and reach the promise of life eternal, through the same Jesus Christ, Your Son, our Lord. Amen.

FOR PATIENCE

Gracious Father, grant us Your Holy Spirit, that in the various and manifold troubles of this life, we would wait patiently for Your deliverance. Be with us in our troubles, and grant us the comfort of Your presence and Your promises. May we follow the example of Your Son, our Lord Jesus Christ, who suffered much before entering into His glory. May we follow Him and come at last to the endless joys of the resurrection, through the same Jesus Christ, our Lord. Amen.

FOR THOSE NEAR DEATH

Lord, have mercy. Christ, have mercy. Lord, have mercy.

Almighty Father, be with Your child _____, whose death draws near. Forgive <u>him/her</u> all <u>his/her</u> sins. Strengthen <u>his/her</u> faith in You and Your promises of life. Comfort <u>him/her</u> with Your Holy Spirit. Keep <u>him/her</u> in Your tender mercy and care. Send Your holy angels to carry <u>him/her</u> into Your presence, that <u>he/she</u> might see the face of Jesus and know the fullness of Your love. Receive <u>him/her</u> by Your mercy into Your glorious kingdom, through Jesus Christ, Your Son, our Lord. Amen.

WHEN DEATH HAS OCCURRED

In life and in death we are Yours, O Lord. Mercifully receive the soul of our beloved into Your blessed kingdom. Give us Your Holy Spirit, that through faith in You we, too, will come to that final resting place. Bless and keep our loved one's mortal remains in safety until the great Last Day of the resurrection, and come quickly, O Lord, that we might know the joys of the life to come. Amen.

FOR THOSE WHO MOURN

Holy Spirit, as we mourn the death of our loved one, comfort us with the sure hope of the resurrection of the body and the life everlasting. Let not our sorrows overcome us. Mix hope and faith with our sorrows and tears. Fix our eyes on Jesus, the author and perfecter of our faith, and give us the sure and certain hope of the resurrection of the body and the life everlasting, through Jesus Christ, Your Son, our Lord. Amen.

THE FUNERAL COLLECT

Lord God, our Shepherd, You gather the lambs of Your flock into the arms of Your mercy and bring them home. Comfort us with the certain hope of the resurrection to everlasting life and a joyful reunion with those we love who have died in the faith; through Jesus Christ, Your Son, our Lord, who lives and reigns with You and the Holy Spirit, one God, now and forever. Amen.

ADDITIONAL RESOURCES

Concordia Publishing House offers many resources for all ages. Visit **www.cph.org** or call **1-800-325-3040** to order.

FOR ADULTS

Deffner, Donald L. *At the Death of a Child.* (14-2029)

Ebeling, Carol Fredericks. *What to Say: 52 Positive Ways to Show Christian Sympathy to Those Who Grieve.* (12-4118)

Just Jr., Arthur A. and Scot Kinnaman. *Visitation: Resources for the Care of Souls.* (15-5097)

Sonnenberg, Roger. *Comfort for Christians.* (20-3726)

Wangerin Jr., Walter. *Confronting Death: A Christian Approach to Life* (DVD). (20-3463)

FOR CHILDREN

Adams, Michelle Medlock. *I Will Not Be Afraid.* (56-2423)

Barker, Peggy. *What Happened When Grandma Died.* (56-1458)

Bohlmann, Katharine. *Grandpa Is There a Heaven?* (56-2126)

Marxhausen, Joanne. *3 in 1: A Picture of God* (56-2291)

———. *Heaven Is a Wonderful Place.* (56-2292)

TRACTS (sold in packs of 25)

Barry, Alvin L. *What about Death and Dying?* (10-1715)

Can You Be Sure of Eternal Life? (10-1743)

Dealing with Death (10-1762)

Making Sense Out of Suffering (10-1787)

Prayers in Bereavement (10-1760)

They Say I'm Dying (10-1784)

PERSONAL INFORMATION

Name: First, Middle, Last

Birthday: mo/day/yr

Address: Street

        City   State   Zip

Phone: Home   Cell   Work

I understand that the information and instructions provided here are for the guidance of my congregation, my family, and my friends for making arrangements necessary at the time of my death. Although this information is being left for safekeeping, it is not legally binding or enforceable. I understand that this worksheet does not make the congregation or my family obliged or responsible for the execution of these instructions.

Signature   Date

Confessing Christ with My Funeral

Jesus says, "Everyone who acknowledges Me before men, I also will acknowledge before My Father who is in heaven" (Matthew 10:32). The Christian delights in confessing the saving name of Jesus before all the world, because it is through the Lord Jesus' death on the cross that we have life and hope and peace. Because of Jesus' death for us, when our last hour comes, we will pass from death to life. Our funeral service is a worship service of the Holy Trinity, who brought us from death to life by the death of Jesus and who has now delivered us from this veil of tears to Himself in heaven. In thanks to God for His gift of eternal life, in planning our funeral we have one final opportunity to make the good confession of our Lord Jesus to men.

What I Would Have My Funeral Service Confess

_____

_____

_____

Scriptures to Confess

Psalm   Why?

_____

_____

_____

Old Testament

_____

_____

_____

_____

Epistle

_____

_____

_____

Gospel

_____

_____

_____

_____

HYMNS TO CONFESS

Name, hymnal, and number   Why?

_____

_____

_____

_____

_____

ADDITIONAL INFORMATION

I have a will. Location: _____

_____

Funeral Home: (preferred company, contact person, phone number)

_____

_____

_____

Prearrangements made for the funeral: (casket, flowers, attire, jewelry, etc.)

_____

_____

_____

_____

Prearrangements made for the burial: (cemetery, plot, tombstone)

_____

_____

_____

_____

FUNERAL PLANNING WORKSHEET

Church: (name, location, phone)

_____

_____

_____

Pallbearers: (including contact information)

- _____
- _____
- _____
- _____
- _____
- _____
- _____
- _____

Church arrangements: (flowers, flag, viewing, etc.)

_____

_____

_____

_____

_____

Memorial gifts:

_____

_____

_____

Notes for the care of the body: (organ donation, embalming, burial, etc.)

_____

_____

_____

Notes and additional thoughts:

_____

_____

_____

_____

Personal History and Information

Birth location:

Baptism date and location (church):

Confirmation   date: church:

                 verse: hymn:

Church membership:

Marriage and Family

Spouse:

Anniversary:

Children

Name

    Phone

    Address

Name

    Phone

    Address

Name

    Phone

    Address

Name

    Phone

    Address

Name

    Phone

    Address

Grandchildren, Great-grandchildren

_____
_____
_____
_____
_____
_____
_____
_____
_____

WORK, ORGANIZATIONS, HOBBIES, MAJOR LIFE EVENTS, AND OTHER INTERESTS
(Years worked, retirement, trips, accomplishments, etc.)

_____
_____
_____
_____
_____
_____
_____
_____
_____
_____
_____
_____
_____
_____
_____
_____
_____

Note: Please attach additional information on a separate sheet. It is also prudent to have a list of the location of all important legal, financial, and personal documents (including birth certificates, marriage license, will, stocks and bonds, titles of property, bank account numbers, insurance policies, etc.).